MAINE COAST
TRAVEL GUIDE
2024/2025

Scenic routes, local flavours and hidden Coastal Treasures

TABLE OF CONTENT

INTRODUCTION

Why Go to the Maine Coast? Why wouldn't you is the actual query. Maine is a state where history and the ocean collide, lighthouses watch over the coastline like ancient sentinels, and fresh adventures await at every morning. Visitors to this location experience a deep sense of serenity, connection, and joy that is difficult to find anywhere.

Imagine waking up to the sight of fishing boats sailing out to sea, the sound of waves softly crashing on the shore, and the scent of salt in the air. This is the Maine Coast, where each day seems like a gift and each instant offer the chance to make lifelong memories.

The remarkable diversity of the Maine Coast is among my favourite things about it. You can find what you're searching for here, whether it's a serene, contemplative getaway or a challenging outdoor experience. With its stunning harbours, remote beaches, and towering cliffs, the coastline is a natural wonder. But the feeling of the Maine Coast is what captivates visitors, not simply the breath-taking beauty. This place exudes a sense of community and permanence, making you feel like a part of something greater than yourself.

The Maine Coast presents countless exploration opportunities for the daring traveller. Enjoy breath-taking vistas while hiking Acadia National Park's coastal paths. Discover undiscovered islands while kayaking through peaceful coves. Alternatively, if you're very daring, take your hand at surfing the Atlantic waves. There are countless methods to raise your heart rate and spirits.

But thrill-seekers aren't the only ones who like the Maine Coast. You can also take your time and enjoy life's small joys there. Take a leisurely afternoon to meander through the quaint streets of Boothbay Harbour or Camden, where one can discover distinctive items at boutique stores and art galleries. Take in the breath-taking vistas and always fresh catch of the day while dining at one of the many seafood restaurants. Enjoy a traditional Maine lobster roll as well—there's nothing quite like it.

The rich history of the Maine Coast is one of its many unique qualities. Whether you're strolling through a town that has managed to hold onto its old-world charm or touring a historic lighthouse, this is a location where the past is ever-present. This place exudes a sense of continuity, as if the tales of the ancestors are still alive and well and just waiting to be uncovered.

The Maine Coast is an endless playground for families. At low tide, kids can explore the tidal pools and find marine life such as crabs and starfish. Enjoy a picnic with a view after a kid-friendly stroll to one of the many lighthouses. Alternatively, spend the day making sandcastles and splashing around in the waves at a sandy beach.

Everyone may find something to like here, and the memories you create will be treasured for a long time.

Not to be overlooked is the beauty of nature. The Maine Coast, with its breath-taking sunsets, foggy mornings, and vivid fall foliage, is a photographer's paradise. This is a great place to discover inspiration if you're an expert with a full camera setup or an amateur with a smartphone. Every bend in the road and every curve in the shoreline presents a different angle and a fresh chance to capture the spirit of this amazing location.

Don't be scared to customize the guide as you explore it. Make your own travel itinerary by using it as a guide, an inspiration source, and a tool. Perhaps you'll choose to spend more time in one location because it appeals to you rather than visiting one of the more popular sights in favour of a peaceful afternoon in a tiny town. Traveling is beautiful since it's as much about the journey as the destination.

Throughout the guide, I've also provided helpful advice to help you avoid typical problems and have the smoothest, most pleasurable travel possible. These suggestions, which range from packing lists to safety guidelines, are meant to give you peace of mind and a sense of readiness as you embark on your journey.

Ultimately, this guide is an invitation rather than merely a compilation of facts. An invitation to explore the charm and beauty of the Maine Coast, to make lifelong memories there, and to uncover its mysteries. So prepare to discover one of the most alluring places on earth by packing your bags, opening your heart, and setting forth. I'm excited to assist you in exploring everything that the Maine Coast has to offer. It is waiting for you.

CHAPTER 2: MAKE TRAVEL PLANS

Choosing Your Travel Objectives

Think about what you really want out of your trip to the Maine Coast before you begin packing your luggage or making travel arrangements. Setting specific travel goals can make all the difference between a good and an amazing holiday, even if it may seem like an easy effort. Consider what most excited you about visiting this stunning area. Do you find great joy in going on outdoor adventures? Maybe the thought of kayaking over calm seas, hiking along craggy coastline trails, or experiencing Acadia National Park's wilderness makes your pulse race. If so, one of your vacation objectives may be to take in as much of Maine's breath-taking scenery as you can.

You might, however, feel more drawn to explore the rich history and culture of the Maine Coast. Are you drawn to the idea of exploring enduring lighthouses, seeing marine museums, or meandering through historic towns? If so, the main focus of your journey can be learning about this area's history and immersing yourself in the customs and tales that have molded it.

It is possible that you require a break from the daily chaos and need a genuine getaway. If your dream vacation involves lounging by the sea, enjoying fresh seafood, and taking leisurely strolls down the beach, then relaxation and rejuvenation may be the main focus of your travel plans. The Maine Coast is, after all, a location to rest, rejuvenate, and reestablish connections with your loved ones as well as places to explore.

The Maine Coast can fulfill your demands, whatever they may be. By specifying the type of experience you want, you can make your travel plan specifically to fulfill your needs. This could entail creating a timetable that is jam-packed with events or leaving plenty of time to unwind and savor the present. For instance, if adventure is your main objective, you may arrange to spend a few days hiking difficult trails and taking in the park's varied scenery. If you're more interested in history and culture, you may design an itinerary that includes stops at some of the many little coastal communities, each with a distinct past to share.

The Maine Coast is beautiful because it has something to offer everyone, and the first step in planning a vacation that is ideal for you is determining your travel objectives. It's okay to mix and match your areas of interest. Maybe you wish to spend your afternoons lounging by the sea and your mornings sightseeing. Alternatively, perhaps you're organizing a family vacation and need to strike a balance between kid-friendly activities and quiet time for yourself. Whatever your circumstances, having specific goals for your trip can help you make the most of your time on the Maine Coast by tailoring it to your interests and preferences with the ideal mix of activities.

Selecting Your Trip Dates

Selecting the ideal time to visit the Maine Coast is the next step after deciding on your vacation objectives. The season you choose might have a significant influence on your experience because timing is crucial. Selecting your visit dates based on your desired sights and activities is crucial because the Maine Coast has something special to offer throughout the year.

Spring (March to May): If you want to avoid the summer crowds, spring is a great season to explore the Maine Coast. After a long winter, the towns come alive as the days become longer and the snow melts, causing the shoreline to burst with wildflowers. Because of the mild weather and quieter routes, this is a perfect time to go trekking. Make sure to bring clothing because the weather can still be chilly, especially in March and the first part of April. As the lobster season begins in the spring, there will be many chances for you to savour locally produced, fresh seafood.

Summer (June to August): With good reason, summer is the busiest season along the Maine Coast. The towns are humming with bustle, the days are long, and the weather is warm. This is the ideal time of year to visit the many festivals held throughout the season, take a boat excursion, or simply enjoy the beaches. But warmer temperatures and lively activities also mean more people and more expensive costs, particularly in well-known locations like Portland and Bar Harbour. Booking your lodging and activities far in advance is a smart idea if you intend to visit during the summer.

Autumn (September to November): There's no doubt that this is the most picturesque season to explore the Maine Coast. The entire shoreline is covered in a vivid tapestry of reds, oranges, and yellows as the leaves change color. The crisp, chilly weather is ideal for outdoor pursuits like trekking and apple picking. Fall is also a more tranquil time to go because the summertime throngs have dispersed but the eateries and stores are still open. Fall is the ideal time of year for photographers to capture the breath-taking views of Maine's coast.

Winter (December to February): If you adore snow-covered vistas and comfortable fireside retreats, winter on the Maine Coast is a magical time of year. Even though many coastal towns close for the winter, there are still many of things to do. Winter sports enthusiasts can enjoy cross-country skiing and snowshoeing at Acadia National Park, etc. Without the summertime throngs, winter is a perfect time to appreciate the peace and quiet of the seaside. Just be ready for chilly weather and the potential for snowfall, and be sure to check ahead for any seasonal closures.

The greatest time to visit the Maine Coast truly depends on what you want to see and do. Each season has its own unique beauty. Based on your travel objectives, this section will walk you through the benefits and drawbacks of each season so you can choose the best time to visit. The Maine Coast will enthral you whether you're drawn to the brilliant intensity of summer, the spectacular splendour of fall, the quiet seclusion of winter, or the new beginnings of spring.

Making Travel Arrangements

After determining the best time to travel, you need to consider how to get there. Whether you're traveling by car from a nearby state or arriving by plane, the Maine Coast is very accessible. If you take the time to appreciate the beautiful routes along the way, the journey itself can become an exciting part of the experience.

Flying: Portland International Jetport (PWM) or Bangor International Airport (BGR) are the best options if you're traveling from a distance. Both airports provide an easy access point to the Maine Coast and are well-connected to major cities throughout the United States. Particularly Portland, with its energetic city centre and close proximity to well-liked coastal communities, is a terrific place to start. However, because Bangor lies nearer the northern coast, it's a great place to start your exploration of Acadia National Park and beyond.

Traveling: Taking a road trip to the Maine Coast is a great way to view the area if you're close enough to drive there. One of the most beautiful drives in the nation is along U.S. Route 1, which stretches from the southernmost point of Maine to the Canadian border. Along the route, there will be many chances to stop and explore as you go through quaint towns and over famous bridges. I absolutely enjoy the flexibility that comes with driving since it lets you to appreciate the beauty of the coast, find hidden gems, and make impromptu detours.

Public Transportation: There are still several ways to get around if you would rather not drive. Train service is available from Boston to a number of locations along the southern Maine Coast via Amtrak Down-easter, including Portland, Freeport, and Brunswick. Once in Maine, you can travel around via rideshares, taxis, and local bus services. Many towns also provide trolley services in the summer, which facilitate simple exploration without a car.

Scenic Drives: Having the chance to stop and enjoy the view while traveling is one of the best things about visiting the Maine Coast. Some of my favourite scenic drives are the one from Ellsworth to Bar Harbour, which provides breath-taking views of Acadia National Park, and the one from Portland to Camden, where you'll pass through charming communities and enjoy breath-taking ocean views. It's important to take your time enjoying these journeys, stopping frequently to take in the scenery, try some fresh seafood, and visit nearby sites.

I'll give you some advice on how to get the most out of your journey along the Maine Coast if you're a sucker for beach road trips. This could include suggestions for the nicest lunch spots, the most picturesque vistas, or the most fascinating side trips. Driving with the windows down, the wind blowing over your hair, and the possibility of adventure lurking around every corner creates a really unique experience.

Advice on Travel Insurance

Travel insurance is undoubtedly one of the most crucial aspects of trip preparation, even though it may not be the most attractive. It's vital to have the assurance that you're covered in case of emergency, particularly while visiting a destination as vibrant as the Maine Coast.

You may avoid unforeseen expenses resulting from medical problems, trip cancellations, misplaced luggage, and more by purchasing travel insurance. It's crucial to be ready for anything, whether your plans involve sailing off the coast, hiking through Acadia National Park, or just savouring the regional food.

Various travel insurance options are available, based on your requirements:

Medical Insurance: This protects you against any unplanned medical costs, including emergency room visits and hospital stays. This is particularly crucial if you're organizing activities with a higher risk of injury, like hiking or kayaking.

Trip Cancellation Insurance: In the event that you have to postpone your vacation due to unanticipated events like illness, natural disasters, or family situations, this insurance type reimburses you for non-refundable costs.

Insurance for Luggage: Should your luggage be misplaced or pilfered

CHAPTER 3: MAINE'S SEASONAL OVERVIEW: WHEN TO VISIT

Best time to visit

The Maine Coast is a location of ageless beauty, with unique experiences to be had in every season. Maine is a destination for all seasons, from the first spring blossoms to the brilliant fall colors, and from the warmth of summer to the serene calm of winter. Knowing what each season has to offer can make it easier for you to decide when to visit and make sure your trip is full of the sights, sounds, and activities that most appeal to you.

Spring: March to May: Rejuvenation and Rebirth

On the Maine Coast, spring has a certain quality. The area seems to come alive after the long, harsh winter. The days are becoming longer, the air is crisp and fresh, and the scenery is starting to change colour. Since spring is a season of rebirth and renewal, it's the best time of year for people to have a more private, tranquil experience of the Maine Coast.

There are still traces of winter in March, as seen by the lower temperatures and chance of snowfall in the northern regions. However, the first clear indications of spring arrive around April. Along the shore, wildflowers start to blossom, and patches of new greens appear in the fields and woodlands. This is the ideal time of year to go hiking because there are fewer people on the trails and the chilly weather makes for comfortable travel. Acadia National Park is especially beautiful in the spring, when its miles of trails and jaw-dropping views come alive.

Seeing the natural world emerge from its winter hibernation is one of the pleasures of traveling in the spring. The return of migrating birds, such as puffins, warblers, and ospreys, will please birdwatchers, and nature lovers will get a kick out of seeing moose, deer, and other species come out of the forests. The coastal waterways also start to brim with life; you may even see whales migrating up the coast or seals sunning themselves on the rocks.

In Maine, the lobster season begins in the spring, and there's no better way to mark your visit than with a delicious fresh lobster roll. Just starting their season, the neighbourhood eateries and fish shacks provide delectable, locally produced meals away from the summertime crush. The essence of spring on the Maine Coast is sitting by the water and savouring a warm, buttery lobster roll while observing the boats bob in the port.

Maine's quaint seaside communities are best explored in the spring, when it's quieter and more serene. You can explore the charming local stores and galleries, take leisurely strolls down the calmer streets, and take advantage of the slower lifestyle that the residents value. Whether you're taking in the serene beauty of Bar Harbour, the artsy communities of Rockland, or the historic streets of Portland, springtime on the Maine Coast offers a more personal and genuine experience.

But be aware that Maine's springtime weather is not always dependable. Rain showers and cold winds are typical, especially in March and the first part of April. The opportunity to witness Maine in all its springtime grandeur, when the scenery is crisp, colourful, and full of promise, is well worth the extra effort of packing layers and waterproof gear.

Summer: The Sun and Sea Season

June to August

The Maine Coast experiences an incredible summer. This is the time of year when the area comes alive, attracting tourists from all over the world who come to enjoy the warm weather, vibrant cities, and limitless outdoor activities the area has to offer. This is the perfect time to visit if you enjoy the sun, the sea, and the bright energy of summer.

During the summer, the beaches are unquestionably the biggest draw. There are several ways to enjoy the coastal waters, such as lounging on the sandy shores of Old Orchard Beach, surfing the waves at Higgins Beach, or exploring the tidal pools at Popham Beach. For a swim on a hot day, the ocean's cool but invigorating temps are ideal. In addition, the summer is the ideal season for paddle boarding, sailing, and kayaking if you enjoy these water sports.

However, it goes beyond the beaches. In addition, summer is festival and event season, with something exciting appearing in every town. There's always a celebration to take part in, from the Maine Lobster Festival in Rockland to the Yarmouth Clam Festival and the Camden Windjammer Festival. These festivals are a great way to experience the local way of life, eat amazing food, and take in live performances of music and entertainment.

A great time to visit Maine's state parks and natural reserves is during the summer. Summertime is the perfect time to explore Acadia National Park, which features breath-taking coastline cliffs, verdant forests, and tranquil lakes. Some of the most stunning scenery in the nation will surround you whether you want to hike up Cadillac Mountain, bike the park's carriage roads, or take a leisurely drive along the Park Loop Road.

Not to be overlooked are the small communities scattered along the Maine coast. These towns are liveliest in the summer, when galleries, restaurants, and stores are humming with bustle. Portland is a great destination to start your summer adventure because of its modern food scene and rich history. Explore the Old Port neighbourhood, go to the Portland Museum of Art, or take a boat to the Casco Bay Islands, which are close by. The quaint communities of Camden, Boothbay Harbour, and Bar Harbor are located further up the coast and each has its own special fusion of culture, history, and scenic beauty.

Summer is, of course, the busiest travel season, which translates into heavier crowds and more expensive travel. It's a good idea to reserve your lodging and activities well in advance if you're going during this time. The adrenaline and excitement of summer on the Maine Coast is simply unrivaled, and the experiences you'll make here will make every second worthwhile, so don't let the popularity put you off.

Autumn: A Visual Delight, September through November

Fall is my favourite season to be on the Maine Coast, if I had to pick. The way the scenery changes—the trees displaying their vibrant fall hues, the air becoming crisp and cool, and the whole area glowing golden—has a certain kind of magic. The fall season begs you to calm down, take deep breaths, and cherish each moment.

The brilliant foliage that covers the hills, woodlands, and coastline throughout the fall season is one of the most recognizable pictures of Maine. The hues contrast spectacularly with the deep blue of the ocean and the beautiful autumn sky, ranging from flaming reds and oranges to warm yellows and golds. Nature's most spectacular show is all around you, whether you're sitting by the sea, driving along the coastal roads, or hiking through the forests.

Because of the cold weather, autumn is also the best season for outdoor activities like riding, hiking, and exploring. Acadia National Park is particularly lovely in the fall, when its trails provide breath-taking vistas of the coastline and surrounding greenery. Whether you're kayaking along the park's untamed shoreline or climbing Cadillac Mountain to see the sunrise, the park's calmer atmosphere in the fall makes for a more serene and introspective experience.

Fall is a season for harvest festivals, apple picking, and all things snug in addition to the beauty of nature. Events like the Common Ground Country Fair, the Fryeburg Fair, and the Damariscotta Pumpkinfest are held in several of the coastal communities to commemorate the season. Enjoy fresh, in-season vegetables, traditional fall fare like apple cider, pumpkin pie, and freshly baked donuts, and learn about the local way of life at these events.

Fall on the Maine Coast is a photographer's and artist's dream. The entire countryside seems to radiate warmth and beauty due to the softer light and richer colors. You'll never run out of ideas, whether you're photographing the beach at sunset, the vibrant trees reflected in a placid lake, or the quaint alleys of a historic town.

Fall travel offers the added benefit of fewer tourists. The stores, eateries, and attractions are still open after the summer visitors have left, making for a more laid-back and unhurried experience. Without the summertime rush, you may leisurely stroll through the charming towns, eat in peace and quiet beside the river, or just take in the local galleries.

It's crucial to remember that autumn weather can be erratic, with temperatures falling swiftly as the season goes on. Packing layers and being ready for a variety of weather conditions, from warm, sunny days to chilly, windy nights, is a good idea. Fall, however, is a truly magical season to see the Maine Coast in all its splendour for those who don't mind a little coolness in the air.

Winter: An Idyll of Peace

From December until February

On the Maine Coast, winter brings with it a calm beauty and beautiful scenery. While many tourists favour the warmer months, winter travellers to Maine are rewarded with a special and serene experience. During the winter, the coast has a whole distinct personality, with snow-covered beaches, frozen lakes, and quaint towns providing a warm haven from the cold.

The Maine Coast offers a wealth of outdoor activities and winter sports for those who enjoy them. During the winter, Acadia National Park is open and offers activities like ice fishing, snowshoeing, and cross-country skiing. The park's carriage roads, which are well-liked by bikers in the summer, transform into a groomed network of miles of paths through the icy woodland for skiers and snowshoers in the winter.

Even though it's cold, the beaches seem beautiful in their winter clothes. It is a stunning and serene sight to see snow-covered dunes and cold waves crashing on the shore. Take a stroll around the beach while wrapped up; you'll probably have

CHAPTER 4: PLANNING YOUR TRAVEL BUDGET

Calculating Travel Expenses

While organizing a trip to the Maine Coast is an exciting endeavour, it is crucial to determine your budget before making any travel or activity plans. By being aware of your financial constraints, you can take advantage of everything the Maine Coast has to offer without being caught off guard. The good news is that Maine is a flexible tourist location that suits travellers on a variety of budgets, from thrifty vacationers to luxury seekers.

Cost of Accommodations: There are many different places to stay along the Maine Coast, from opulent beachfront resorts to quaint bed & breakfasts and affordable motels. High-end accommodations can set you back anywhere from $300 to $600 a night if you're looking to splurge, especially during the busiest times of the year. These opulent lodgings frequently have breath-taking views, on-site restaurants, and first-rate extras like spas and private beaches.

There are many mid-range hotels, motels, and inns with nightly rates between $150 and $300 for those on a more modest budget. These choices frequently offer a warm and inviting stay with the extra allure of regional hospitality. Numerous of these hotels and motels are found in charming towns, making it simple to get to neighbouring sights and restaurants.

Even with a limited budget, there are still lots of reasonably priced options for travel. Motels, hostels, and even campgrounds that are affordable have overnight rates ranging from $50 to $150. With several campgrounds situated close to beaches, forests, and parks, camping in particular may be an affordable and unforgettable way to take in the natural beauty of the Maine Coast.

Costs associated with Dining: The Maine Coast is a foodie's paradise, but you don't have to go broke enjoying your culinary explorations. Spend between $50 and $100 per person at upmarket restaurants if you're in the mood for gourmet dining, where you can savour Maine's signature seafood, locally produced products, and creative cuisine. These restaurants often feature elegant settings and waterfront views, making for a truly special dining experience.

For a more casual supper, you may find plenty of selections at local diners, pubs, and seafood shacks, with average rates ranging from $15 to $30 per person. Savour a traditional lobster roll, a mainstay of Maine's food scene, which usually costs $15 to $25, depending on the place and the size of the roll. Don't miss this opportunity.

If you're on a budget, you can save money by checking out local markets, bakeries, and delis, where you can pick up fresh, cheap meals for $10 or less. Farmers' markets are another feature of many communities. Here you may purchase locally grown produce, cheeses, and baked products to put together your own picnic, which is a fun way to eat outside amid the breath-taking scenery of Maine.

Activities and Attractions: There are a ton of free or inexpensive activities and attractions along the Maine Coast. Exploring state parks, hiking trails, and beaches is often free or requires only a minor parking fee (usually $5 to $15 per vehicle). Visiting lighthouses, walking through old villages, and taking in the coastline views are also free and offer some of the most memorable moments of your trip.

For paid attractions, such as museum admissions, boat tours, or guided hikes, you may expect to spend anywhere from $10 to $50 per person, depending on the activity. Whale watching cruises, which are a major attraction along the Maine Coast, normally cost between $40 and $70 per person, but they offer an amazing experience of viewing these magnificent creatures up close.

Transportation prices: Transportation prices can vary based on how you want to travel. If you're flying into Maine, add in the cost of flight, which can range widely based on your departure city and the time of year. The most practical method to see the coast of Maine is by automobile, with daily rental prices varying from $40 to $100, depending on the type of vehicle and the time of year.

Although Maine's gas prices are normally in line with the national average, if you intend to travel long distances along the coast, you need budget more for fuel. Public transit alternatives include buses and the Amtrak Downeaster rail, which travels from Boston to a number of communities along the southern Maine Coast, if you would rather not drive. These are less expensive options, with one-way costs usually between $10 and $30.

Shopping and souvenirs: You can be as frugal or as extravagant as you wish when it comes to your Maine Coast shopping. Unique souvenirs can be more expensive in high-end boutiques, art galleries, and specialized shops, but more reasonably priced options can be found in local markets and craft festivals. Depending on your interests and the kinds of things you want to buy for your home, budget anywhere from $20 to $200 for your shopping trip.

Reducing Travel Expenses

You may enjoy the Maine Coast's offerings without going over budget if you plan ahead and travel, which doesn't have to be pricey. Here are some insider suggestions to help you maximize your budget and stretch your money.

Select the Appropriate Time to Visit: Selecting the appropriate time to visit is one of the simplest methods to save money. The most expensive months to visit the Maine Coast are June through August, when demand is highest for lodging, dining, and activities. If your schedule is flexible, think about going in late spring (May) or early fall (September to October), which the shoulder seasons. There will be less crowds, cheaper pricing, and plenty of lovely weather during these periods.

Look for Deals and Discounts: Take some time to look for deals and discounts before to making travel arrangements. Special rates are available for last-minute reservations, extended stays, and travel during off-peak times at many hotels, inns, and campgrounds. Discounts on lodging, food, and activities can frequently be found on websites such as Group on, Travel zoo, and regional tourism boards.

Utilize your travel discounts if you're a member of groups like AAA or AARP. You can save money on everything from hotel to auto rentals. Inquire about any possible discounts as well; a lot of museums and attractions offer reduced prices for families, elderly, or students.

Eat Wisely: While dining out might be one of the biggest travel expenses, there are ways to savour Maine's cuisine without going over budget. If possible, try to eat your major meal during lunch, when many restaurants serve cheaper versions of the same meals that are served at supper. Look for early bird deals or prix fixe menus that provide numerous courses at a lower fee.

Buying fresh picnic foods at your neighbourhood farmers' market or grocery shop is another excellent method to save money. This is not only an affordable alternative, but it also lets you eat in some of the most picturesque locations along the shore. Imagine enjoying a peaceful beachside meal or gazing out over a charming harbour while nibbling on fresh bread, regional cheese, and in-season fruit.

Benefit from Free and Cheap Activities:

The Maine Coast offers a wealth of natural beauty, and many of the best things to do here are inexpensive or free. Beachcombing along the coast, hiking in Acadia National Park, and touring the charming villages are all inexpensive or free activities. If you bring along an adventurous spirit and comfortable shoes, you'll discover that some of your trip's most treasured experiences will cost you nothing at all.

Many communities provide free or inexpensive cultural experiences, such outdoor concerts, art walks, and community events, in addition to their natural features. Look for any festivals or get-togethers on the local event calendars while you're there; they can be great low-cost ways to fully immerse yourself in the culture of the area.

Examine Cost-Effective Lodging Choices:

Although opulent resorts and boutique motels may entice you, there exist numerous reasonably priced accommodations that provide coziness and allure. Search for reasonably priced motels, inns, or bed & breakfasts that offer comfortable, well-maintained lodging at a significantly lower price. A different choice is to book a stay on Airbnb or a vacation rental; in these cases, you may frequently find larger accommodations for families or groups at a cheaper cost per person.

If you love the great outdoors, camping can be a cheap and exciting way to see the Maine Coast. Numerous campgrounds provide sites with stunning views, handy access to parks and beaches, and conveniences like picnic areas and showers. Additionally, camping enables you to savor the basic joys of a starry night and establish a connection with the natural world.

Tools for Budget Planning

Now that you have an idea of how much your trip will cost and know some money-saving tips, it's time to plan. You can remain within your budget, locate the best discounts, and keep track of your spending by using budget planning tools. Here are a few of my top tools and apps to assist you with budgeting for your trip.

TripIt: TripIt is an all-in-one trip planner that assists you in keeping track of all your travel arrangements. It is mainly used for itinerary planning, but it also offers tools that let you keep track of your spending. You can enter your vacation budget, keep an eye on your expenditures, and check to see if your expenses match your budget. It's an excellent tool for managing your money and making sure everything goes according to plan when traveling.

❖ **Mint:**

If you're looking to manage your vacation budget, Mint is a well-known personal finance tool. You may use it to track your spending, create a budget, and get alerts when you're about to go over your spending limit. You can see where your money is going and make any modifications by classifying your spending (lodging, food, entertainment, etc.).

❖ **Trail Wallet:**

Specifically created to assist you in managing your expenses while traveling, Trail Wallet is a budgeting tool. It lets you categorize your expenses, track your spending in real time, and establish a daily budget. One of my favorite aspects is the capacity to

CHAPTER 5: MAINE COAST ESSENTIALS FOR TRAVELERS' PACKING LIST

The excitement of packing for a trip is one of its best parts; it involves organizing your clothes, dreaming of future excursions, and making sure you're ready for anything that may arise. The Maine Coast necessitates careful packing due to its wide range of activities and unpredictable weather. Making the most of your trip is certain whether you're hiking in Acadia National Park, exploring quaint coastal villages, or spending a day at the beach.

Apparel for Every Season: Since Maine's weather is erratic, it's critical to bring layers of clothing for all scenarios. It can be chilly in the mornings and nights, especially by the seaside, even in the summer, so dressing in layers will help you be comfortable all day.

Base Layers: If you're going to be active, start with base layers that wick away moisture to keep you comfortable and dry. The best materials are lightweight, breathable ones like synthetic mixes or merino wool.

Mid Layers: Pack a few mid-layer garments, including light sweaters or fleece jackets. These are necessary for staying warm in the early morning or late at night and can be added or removed based on the temperature.

Outer Layers: A windproof and waterproof jacket is essential because Maine is renowned for its unexpected downpours of rain. To make it easy to bring with you in a daypack, look for something that is lightweight and packable. Additionally useful is a rain poncho, particularly if you intend to go out and about in bad weather.

Pants and Shorts: Bring a variety of pants and shorts, depending on the season. While casual shorts or capris are a terrific choice for warm, sunny days, quick-drying, comfy hiking pants are a great choice for outdoor activities.

Shoes: One of the most crucial things to remember to pack for the Maine Coast is shoes. For traction and ankle support, you must wear strong hiking boots or trail shoes if you intend to hike or explore the rocky shoreline. Bring water shoes or sandals that are comfy and can withstand both water and sand for your beach days. Additionally, remember to bring along some comfy, casual shoes for exploring the town.

Swimwear: It's still advisable to pack a swimsuit even if you're not going during the summer. Indoor pools and hot tubs are common at hotels and resorts, and adventurous people may even brave an ocean swim (though the water is very cold!).

Accessory items: Even on chilly days, a broad-brimmed hat, sunglasses, and an effective sunscreen are essential for shielding oneself from the sun's rays. For added warmth or sun protection, a lightweight scarf or bandana might be helpful. Additionally, a decent daypack is vital for transporting your belongings on day travels.

What to Pack for a Certain Activity:

Trekking & Outdoor Adventures: If you're going on an outdoor adventure, don't forget to pack a map of the area you'll be trekking in, a hydration system or water bottles, and a compass or GPS device. For more difficult hikes, trekking poles might be useful, and bringing a first aid kit is usually a good idea. Be sure to have a sturdy tent, a comfortable sleeping bag, and cooking supplies if you intend to go camping.

Beach Days: Bring a beach towel, a foldable beach chair or blanket, and a cooler with snacks and beverages for those bright days by the water. Bring beach toys and a book or magazine for some leisurely reading if you're going with children.

Photography: If you enjoy taking pictures, bring along your camera, additional batteries, and memory cards. The Maine Coast is a photographer's dream. When taking long-exposure pictures of the surf or those stunning sunsets, a tripod can come in handy.

Binoculars: These are a terrific addition to your packing list if you enjoy observing whales or birds. One of the great draws of Maine is its unique wildlife, and bringing binoculars along will make the experience even better.

Maine's Changing Weather: Because of its maritime climate, which is subject to sudden changes, it is imperative to pack accordingly. Summertime temperatures can vary from the upper 50s to the low 80s, but spring and fall may offer more unpredictable, colder weather. If you plan to visit during the cold, snowy winter months, remember to bring warm, insulating layers, gloves, a hat, and a heavy coat.

Rain Gear: As previously shown, the Maine Coast is always susceptible to rain. If you anticipate being outside in the rain, remember to bring an umbrella and waterproof pants in addition to your waterproof jacket. Investing in waterproof bags or covers for your valuables and electronics is also a smart move.

Cool Weather Gear: The evenings may get chilly even in the summer. Bring a thick fleece or sweater, and for those who are more susceptible to the cold, don't forget to bring a cap and gloves. These will be necessities in the fall and spring.

When packing for a winter trip, keep warmth as your top priority. You'll stay warm with thermal base layers, heavy socks, insulated boots, and a premium down or synthetic jacket. In addition, gloves, a hat, a scarf, and hand and foot warmers are essential on really chilly days.

No matter when you visit, you can make the most of the Maine Coast by planning ahead and packing carefully for a variety of weather scenarios.

Tips for Health and Safety

Your safety is the first priority, and you can make sure your trip to the Maine Coast is both pleasurable and safe by being ready for its particular challenges. The following are some vital safety and health advice specific to the area:

Water Safety: The Maine Coast is highly prioritized because to its breath-taking beaches, untamed coasts, and numerous waterways.

Swimming: The Maine coast's Atlantic Ocean is stunning, but it can also be chilly and erratic. Always be aware of any local swimming advisories and keep an eye out for warning flags that are displayed at beaches. Even in the summer, the water can be frigid, and particularly on open ocean beaches, there may be powerful currents called riptides. Never swim alone and only go in the approved areas where lifeguards are on duty.

Kayaking and Boating: Regardless of your swimming skill, wear a life jacket if you plan to spend any time on the water, be it kayaking, paddle boarding, or boating. Check the weather forecast before leaving, and be mindful of the tides and currents, which can vary quickly. Because coastal fog can move in swiftly and reduce visibility, it's critical to be organized and have a strategy for returning to shore.

Hypothermia: If you're not clothed appropriately or spend too much time in the water, the cold water can cause hypothermia even in the warmer months. Consider donning a wetsuit if you're going to be in the water for a prolonged amount of time when participating in water sports.

Precautions for Wildlife:

Although encounters with Maine's diverse fauna are usually harmless, it's still advisable to take steps to prevent uninvited contact.

Bears: Keep in mind that black bears can be found in Maine if you plan to hike or camp in more isolated locations, especially inland. Store all food and scented goods away from your campsite, preferably in a bear-proof container or hung from a tree, to prevent them from attracting bears. If you come across a bear, stay composed, enlarge yourself, and retreat gradually. Avoid running as this can lead to a pursuit reaction.

Moose: Although gorgeous, moose may be dangerous, particularly in the fall when they breed. When driving or trekking, stay well away from moose and avoid approaching them. If they sense danger, deer may turn hostile.

Ticks: Ticks are prevalent in Maine, especially in regions with grass or woods, and some of them may be carriers of Lyme disease. Wear long sleeves and pants, apply DEET-containing insect repellent, and thoroughly check oneself for ticks after being outside as precautions. If a tick is discovered, remove it right away with tweezers, making sure to grab it as near to the skin as you can.

❖ Local Emergency Services

It's critical to understand how to contact local services in an emergency.

❖ Emergency Numbers

If you need police, fire, or medical assistance in Maine, call 911. Always carry a fully charged phone, particularly when traveling to far-flung locations.

❖ Hospitals and Clinics

Learn where the closest hospitals and clinics are located in the areas you'll be visiting. While there are tiny medical facilities in many coastal villages, larger hospitals can handle more serious ailments and are found in places like Portland, Bangor, and Brunswick.

Pharmacies:

You can get prescriptions filled and over-the-counter drugs in most communities' at least one pharmacy. Bring a list of local pharmacies along with their hours of operation if you have any special medical needs.

CHAPTER 6: REQUIREMENTS FOR ENTRY AND VISAS

Visa Processing

E xciting adventures can be had when visiting the stunning Maine Coast from outside the US, but before you leave, make sure all of your entry and visa requirements are met. Although navigating the visa application procedure may seem overwhelming, you can guarantee a seamless and stress-free admission into the United States with the correct knowledge and a little bit of planning. I'll walk you through every step of this process in this chapter, from figuring out whether you need a visa to getting ready to go through customs and immigration.

Who Requires a Visa?

Find out if you require a visa in order to enter the United States before you begin packing your luggage and making your travel schedule. Depending on your country, the reason for your travel, and the length of your stay, different restrictions apply.

Visa Waiver Program (VWP): For brief stays lasting up to 90 days, citizens of the 40 nations that take part in the program may not require a visa to enter the United States. For visitors and business travelers who want to enter the United States for a brief time without having to deal with the inconvenience of applying for a visa, this program is perfect. You must still get authorization through the Electronic System for Travel Authorization (ESTA) before to your trip, even if you qualify for the VWP.

You can check the ESTA website or the official U.S. Department of State website to determine if your nation is included in the Visa Waiver Program. Among the nations that are a part of the VWP are the UK, Australia, Japan, France, and Germany.

To apply for an ESTA, go to the website and fill out the online form. It is a simple process that typically takes 20 minutes. Basic details about you, your trip itinerary, and your eligibility under the VWP must be provided.

Cover the Cost: The ESTA application carries a nominal cost, which can be settled online using a credit or debit card.

Await Approval: Although clearance is usually granted in a matter of minutes, it is advised that you apply at least 72 hours before to your departure. Your ESTA is valid for two years after it is authorized or until the expiration of your passport, whichever comes first.

Non-VWP Nations: You will require to apply for a visa before to your trip if you are traveling from a nation that is not included in the Visa Waiver Program.

Tourist Visa (B-2): A B-2 Tourist Visa is required if you're traveling to the Maine Coast for leisure, a holiday, or to see friends and family. With this visa, your maximum stay in the United States is six months; however, the immigration officer at the port of entry will decide how long you can stay.

Business Visa (B-1): You must apply for a B-1 Business Visa if you want to go to the United States for business purposes, such as attending conferences, meetings, or contract negotiations.

Additionally, this visa is valid for up to six months, based on the purpose of your travel.

Student Visa (F-1/M-1): You must apply for an F-1 (academic) or M-1 (vocational) student visa if you intend to study in the United States. These visas are granted for the length of your academic program, with the possibility of an extension for hands-on training.

Various Visas: Work visas (H-1B, L-1), exchange guest visas (J-1), and fiancé visas (K-1) are among the various visa categories for specific purposes. Make sure the visa you seek for corresponds with the reason for your visit.

The Visa Application Process

Although it may appear difficult, applying for a U.S. visa can be a doable procedure if you prepare beforehand. To assist you in navigating the visa application procedure, here is a step-by-step guide:

Step 1: Choose the Kind of Visa You Require Depending on why you are visiting, the first step is to ascertain the kind of visa you require. The majority of travellers, as previously said, will apply for a B-2 Tourist Visa; however, be sure to choose the appropriate visa type based on your intended itinerary.

Step 2: Fill out Form DS-160. The typical online application form for non-immigrant visas is DS-160. This form must be completed on the Consular Electronic Application Centre (CEAC) website run by the U.S. Department of State. The DS-160 form requests extensive details regarding your past, your trip itinerary, and the reason for your stay. Make careful to provide truthful and accurate answers to all queries.

You will receive a confirmation page with a barcode after completing the form. You will need this paper printed out for your visa interview.

Step 3: Cover the Application Fee for a Visa You will be required to pay the non-refundable visa application cost upon the submission of your DS-160 form. The application fee for most business and tourist visas is approximately $160, though it varies based on the type of visa you're seeking for. Depending on the U.S. embassy or consulate in your nation, payments can be paid online or at specified payment locations.

Step 4: Arrange the Interview for Your Visa The next step is to make an appointment for an interview at the American embassy or consulate in your nation of origin. Arranging your appointment as early as feasible is a smart idea because wait periods for interviews can vary. Wait times may be longer during the busiest travel seasons, so make plans appropriately.

Step 5: Compile the Necessary Records Get all the paperwork you'll need to support your visa application before your interview. These could consist of:

A current passport that will still be valid for at least six months after your intended stay in the country.

The confirmation page for DS-160.

The receipt for the visa application fee.

a current passport-sized photo that satisfies the requirements for the photo on a U.S. visa.

Proof of work, family links, or property ownership are examples of evidence demonstrating your ties to your nation of origin.

Information about your travel arrangements, such as your itinerary, hotel bookings, and ticket for the return flight.

any additional paperwork that relates to your visa category, like an invitation letter, evidence of funds, or an employment letter.

Step 6: Go to the Interview for a Visa Bring all necessary documentation to the embassy or consulate on the day of your interview. The interview is an important step in the visa application process since it gives the consular officer a chance to determine if you qualify for a visa. You might be questioned about your trip itinerary, your ties to your home nation, and the purpose of your journey to the United States during the interview.

Be truthful and succinct in your responses. Based on your interview, your documentation, and your general eligibility under U.S. immigration law, the consular official will make a decision. The processing time may increase in some circumstances if more administrative processing is needed.

Step 7: Get your visa The consular official will retain your passport in order to issue the visa if your application is accepted. Although processing periods differ, you should typically receive your passport with the visa stamped in a few days to a few weeks. You can begin organizing your trip to the Maine Coast as soon as you have your visa!

Should your visa application be rejected, you will be provided with a reason for the rejection and, if necessary, instructions on how to reapply.

Advice and Tips for Entering

There are a few crucial considerations to make while entering the US, even if you don't require a visa. There are various procedures involved in entering the country, from immigration and customs inspections to being aware of your rights and obligations as a guest. The following information will help to guarantee a seamless admission into the nation:

Customs and Immigration: Before you may enter the United States, you must pass through customs and immigration when you arrive. This is what to anticipate:

Immigration Check: An immigration official will check your passport, visa (if needed), and ESTA (if applicable) after you arrive. The officer may inquire about your intended itinerary, reason for visiting, and length of stay in the United States. Provide a straightforward and sincere response.

Customs Declaration: You must pick up your bags and pass through customs after clearing immigration. A customs declaration form that inquires about the goods you are bringing into the nation must be filled out by you. Understand the rules set forth by US customs regarding goods that are prohibited, including specific foods, plants, and large quantities of currency. Declare the item and get advice from the customs officer if you're not sure.

❖ Biometric Information:

The United States may request biometric information from visitors, such as a photo and fingerprints, as part of the admission procedure. The majority of foreign tourists must go through this normal process.

❖ Documents to Bring

It's crucial to have a few essential documents on hand when you enter the United States, even if you qualify for the Visa Waiver Program:

❖ Passport

In order for you to enter the United States, your passport must be valid for at least six months. Verify that it's conveniently accessible and in good shape.

ESTA Approval: Print a copy of your ESTA approval and bring it with you if you're traveling under the VWP. Even though it's not always necessary, having it on hand is beneficial in case anything goes wrong.

CHAPTER 7: OVERVIEW OF THE 5-DAY ITINERARY

Fun time

It can be thrilling and intimidating to plan the ideal trip to the Maine Coast, especially if you want to make sure you don't miss any of the must-see sights. The Maine Coast offers so much to explore—whether it breath-taking scenery, quaint towns, or limitless chances for adventure—that it can be difficult to know where to begin. For this reason, I have designed a 5-day itinerary that guarantees you will experience the greatest sights, flavours, and activities in this stunning location.

Whether you're visiting the Maine Coast for the first time or coming back to explore new places, this itinerary is made to provide you with a comprehensive experience of the region. You can experience a mix of unhurried moments, cultural immersion, and outdoor exploration to fully appreciate what makes this area unique. Even though each day has a set schedule, you have ample freedom to go at your own speed or customize the experience.

This itinerary covers the famous locations that define the Maine Coast, from the thriving food scene and rich history of Portland to the untamed beauty of Acadia National Park. To find undiscovered treasures and local favourites that will make your trip genuinely unforgettable, it also deviates from the usual route. This schedule makes sure you see everything the Maine Coast has to offer, whether you're hiking beautiful trails, enjoying delicious seafood by the sea, or touring charming coastal villages.

Day 1: Getting to Know Portland and Seeing the City

The largest city in Maine and the ideal starting point for seeing the state's distinct fusion of urban charm and seaside beauty is Portland, where your journey will begin. Upon arrival, spend some time getting settled in to your lodging, whether it's a quaint bed & breakfast on the waterfront or a small boutique hotel in the Old Port neighbourhood.

Visiting the Old Port District in the morning Take a leisurely stroll through Portland's Old Port neighbourhood to start the day. This historic waterfront area is home to 19th-century brick buildings, cobblestone streets, and a vibrant environment. Portland's retail, dining, and entertainment hub is located here. Take a look around the neighbourhood's specialty stores, art galleries, and boutiques to discover everything from artisanal delicacies to handcrafted jewellery.

Lunch: Savouring the Cuisine of Portland Lunch at one of Portland's highly recommended restaurants is a great way to experience the city's great culinary scene. Portland has a wide variety of food options, including farm-to-table, international, and fresh seafood. I suggest checking out Central Provisions for their inventive take on small meals or Eventide Oyster Co. for their renowned brown butter lobster wrap.

Visit to the Portland Museum of Art in the afternoon Visit the Portland Museum of Art after lunch to view a wide range of American and European artwork by masters including Claude Monet, Edward Hopper, and Winslow Homer. The museum's architecture, which combines modern and old styles, is just as stunning as the artwork it displays.

Evening: Portland Head Light at dusk Visit the recognizable Portland Head Light, which is situated in neighbouring Cape Elizabeth, to cap off your first day. One of the most photographed lighthouses in the country is this ancient lighthouse, which was built in 1791. The vistas are just stunning as the sun sets over the Atlantic. Savour a serene stroll around the cliffs and spend some time exploring Fort Williams Park, which is the area surrounding the lighthouse.

Day 2: Kennebunkport Exploration and Coastal Drive

You will embark on a magnificent road trip along the southern Maine coast on your second day, with a destination of the charming village of Kennebunkport. This region is well-known for its breath-taking beaches, quaint town atmosphere, and historic homes.

Morning: Take a scenic drive Along the US Route 1 Take a trip along U.S. Route 1, which offers stunning views of the coast and lots of places to stop and explore, to start your day. You'll pass through charming communities like Biddeford, Scarborough, and Old Orchard Beach along the route. Every town has a distinct charm of its own, so enjoy the ride and take your time.

Lunch is in Kennebunkport's Dock Square. Reach the center of Kennebunkport's dining and shopping district, Dock Square, by lunchtime after arriving. Explore the neighborhood's boutiques, galleries, and gift shops here. I suggest having lunch at The Clam Shack, a well-known local restaurant that serves fresh seafood. Try their lobster roll, it's delicious!

Walks and a river cruise in the afternoon Enjoy a leisurely stroll along Ocean Avenue after lunch, which provides breathtaking views of the Atlantic Ocean and the rocky shoreline. The Bush family's vacation residence, Walker's Point, is reachable by this picturesque path. Take a river tour along the Kennebunk River to see Kennebunkport from a different angle. These tours provide a leisurely means of taking in the area's historical sites and scenic landscapes from the water.

Dinner at Kennebunkport in the evening Dine at one of Kennebunkport's many excellent restaurants as night falls. The White Barn Inn is a great option for a special occasion because it has a lovely menu with locally sourced ingredients and a romantic atmosphere. Enjoy the peaceful ambiance by strolling along the riverfront after supper.

Day 3: The Adventures of Camden and Penobscot Bay

On the third day, you go even farther up the coast to Camden, a charming town tucked away between the sea and the mountains. Camden, known as the "Jewel of the Maine Coast," is an ideal destination for those who enjoy the great outdoors and the natural world.

Camden Hills State Park in the morning Visit Camden Hills State Park first thing in the morning to trek up to the summit of Mount Battie. The modest hike provides breath-taking views of Penobscot Bay, Camden Harbour, and the neighbouring islands. One of the most famous views on the Maine Coast is the panoramic view from the summit, which is particularly lovely in the early morning hours.

Lunch: Harborside Picnic Return to Camden after your hike and get a picnic lunch from a nearby bakery or deli. A well-liked option that provides a selection of salads, sandwiches, and pastries is the Camden Deli. Bring your lunch outside to the port so you may eat while admiring the boats and the glittering water.

Schooner sailing on Penobscot Bay in the afternoon One of the joys of any vacation to Camden is sailing in Penobscot Bay aboard a historic schooner. These stately wooden ships offer a look into Maine's nautical heritage and provide a calm opportunity to explore the bay's islands and wildlife. Many schooner trips run two to three hours, allowing you plenty of time to relax and take in the gorgeous landscape.

Evening: Camden stroll and dinner In the late afternoon, head back to Camden and take some time to peruse the galleries and stores there. Treat yourself to dinner at Natalie's, which is housed inside the Camden Harbour Inn. The restaurant specializes in modern New England cuisine and provides a quality dining experience. After supper, stroll around the waterfront or stop by a neighbourhood bar for a few drinks.

"Day 4: Exploring Bar Harbour and Acadia National Park"

One of the most stunning and varied national parks in the country, Acadia National Park, is a must-see when visiting the Maine Coast. On the fourth day, spend time discovering this natural marvel. Then, spend the evening in the quaint town of Bar Harbor.

Morning: See the Top Attractions in Acadia To make the most of your time at Acadia National Park, start your day early. Start your visit by taking a drive along the 27-mile Park Loop Road, which leads to many of the park's most well-known locations, such as Sand Beach, Thunder Hole, and Otter Cliff. Make sure to make a stop at Jordan Pond so you can trek the Jordan Pond Path or enjoy a stroll along the coast.

Jordan Pond House for lunch Visit the Jordan Pond House for lunch; it's well-known for its popovers and tea served on the lawn with views of the Bubble Mountains and Jordan Pond. This is a classic Acadia experience and a wonderful way to unwind before venturing further into your trip.

Cadillac Mountain and hiking in the afternoon Explore one of the park's several hiking paths throughout the afternoon. The Beehive Trail, which offers breathtaking views of the park and an exhilarating climb with iron rungs and ladders, is perfect for those who are up for a challenge. The Ocean Path, which provides stunning views of the coastline and access to multiple picturesque overlooks, is a great option for a more moderate climb.

The highest peak on the US East Coast, Cadillac Mountain, should be visited before departing Acadia. When the sun sets and golden light covers the islands and ocean, it is a truly spectacular event that you may witness from the summit if you time your visit well.

Evening: Bar Harbour Head to Bar Harbour after a day of outdoor exploration so you can relax with dinner at one of the many eateries in the area. There are many different types of dining establishments in Bar Harbour, from fancy restaurants to more laid-back seafood shacks. For a fantastic lobster mac & cheese and a laid-back environment, try Side Street Café.

Wander the Shore Path, a beautiful trail that hugs Frenchman Bay's edge, after supper. The trail is a great way to end the day because it provides stunning views of the port and the Porcupine Islands.

Day 5: Departure and Coastal Exploration

Enjoy the last bits of your journey and take in any last-minute sight-seeing on your last day on the Maine Coast.

Morning: Schoodic Peninsula visit Visit the Schoodic Peninsula, the only portion of Acadia National Park, to begin your day.

CHAPTER 8: LODGINGS & HOTELS

Luxury hotels and Affordable

One of the most crucial parts of organizing your trip to the Maine Coast is figuring out where to stay. Travellers looking for a magnificent hideaway, a comfortable yet affordable stay, or a charming inn with a personal touch will find that the Maine Coast has a wide range of lodgings to choose from. I'll present you to some of the top lodging options in this chapter, ranging from opulent, five-star hotels to quaint, reasonably priced inns and resorts. Your visit to the Maine Coast will be memorable and pleasurable no matter which of these lodgings you choose to stay in because I have personally selected them all based on their quality, location, and level of service.

Luxury lodgings along the Maine coast

Some of New England's most exquisite and opulent hotels may be found along the Maine Coast, perfect for indulging when the mood strikes. These properties offer you the ideal environment for rest and relaxation in elegance by fusing first-rate amenities with breath-taking settings. These five-star hotels will make your trip to Maine really unforgettable, whether you're visiting for a particular event or just want to take advantage of everything the state has to offer.

The Auberge Resorts Collection's White Barn Inn

Phone: (207) 967-2321; Address: 37 Beach Avenue, Kennebunk, ME 04043

The White Barn Inn is a 150-year-old, luxurious hotel with a rich history that is tucked away in the quaint town of Kennebunk. Many of the hotel's well furnished rooms and suites have large soaking tubs and fireplaces. Located in a tastefully renovated barn, the on-site restaurant is well-known for its delicious food and charming atmosphere. The hotel also has a spa with a variety of soothing treatments that are available to guests.

The Camden Harbour Hotel

Phone: +1 207-236-4200; Address: 83 Bay View Street, Camden, ME 04843.

With a view of the charming Camden Harbor, Camden Harbour Inn provides a posh and cozy lodging option. This boutique hotel is renowned for its tasteful furnishings, attentive service, and breath-taking views of the mountains and port. Natalie's, the hotel's fine dining establishment, specializes in serving modern New England cuisine made with locally sourced, fresh ingredients. The Camden Harbour Inn is an ideal option for a romantic retreat because of its excellent location and opulent amenities.

Maine Cliff House

Phone: +1 207-361-1000; Address: 591 Shore Road, Cape Neddick, ME 03902

With its stunning vistas and opulent lodging, Cliff House Maine is perched on the brink of the Atlantic Ocean. This contemporary resort offers large rooms with floor to ceiling windows, separate balconies, and tasteful decor. Several on-site dining options, a full-service spa, and an infinity pool with an ocean view are among the hotel's attractions. Cliff House Maine offers an opulent coastal getaway, whether you're dining al fresco, unwinding by the pool, or getting a spa treatment.

The Press Hotel, Collection Autograph

Phone: (207) 807-808-8800; Address: 119 Exchange Street, Portland, ME 04101

The Press Hotel, which offers a mix of elegance and history, is situated in the centre of Portland's downtown. The hotel, which occupies the former Portland Press Herald headquarters, offers chic rooms that are influenced by the building's newspaper history. Local artwork, handcrafted furnishings, and thoughtful extras adorn each room. UNION, the hotel's restaurant, offers farm-to-table fare in a stylish, modern environment. For those who like to experience Portland's thriving eating and arts scenes while remaining in opulence, The Press Hotel is the ideal choice.

Low-Cost Hotels and Hostels

Budget travel doesn't have to mean sacrificing charm or comfort. There are many of inexpensive lodging options on the Maine Coast that provide excellent value without sacrificing quality. These choices will enable you to travel with less money while still having an enjoyable stay, whether you're searching for a family-friendly inn, a modest motel close to the beach, or a comfortable bed & breakfast.

The Acadia Hotel

Address: Bar Harbor, ME 04609, 98 Eden Street

Telephone: (207) 288-3500

Situated in close proximity to Acadia National Park and downtown Bar Harbor, the Acadia Inn provides reasonably priced, cozy lodging options. The hotel offers free breakfast, a heated outdoor pool, and roomy accommodations. It's a great starting point for discovering Acadia's natural beauty and Bar Harbor's charm, and it's close to restaurants, stores, and hiking trails.

The Colonial Hotel

Phone: +1 207-646-5191; Address: 145 Shore Road, Ogunquit, ME 03907

The Colonial Inn, which is located in the charming village of Ogunquit, provides a fusion of contemporary conveniences with antique beauty. This inexpensive inn is conveniently close to Ogunquit's downtown, the Marginal Way, and the ocean. This historic New England inn offers free breakfast, an outdoor pool, and a warm, friendly ambiance to its guests. For tourists who want to take advantage of Ogunquit's attractions without breaking the bank, it's a fantastic option.

Best Dining Options on the Maine Coast

Fresh seafood, farm-to-table cooking, and quaint dining venues that showcase the area's rich culinary legacy are all well-known features of the Maine Coast. The Maine Coast has a wide range of eateries to suit any taste, whether you're searching for a classy dining experience, a quiet cafe, or a casual lobster shack. We'll look at some of the best eateries along the shore in this part; each one offers a distinctive flavour of Maine's culinary gems.

Portland's Eventide Oyster Co.

Phone: (207) 774-8538; Address: 86 Middle Street, Portland, ME 04101

For seafood enthusiasts, Eventide Oyster Co. in Portland is a must-visit. This restaurant has a contemporary, lively ambiance and is well-known for its creative twists on traditional New England fare as well as its fresh, locally sourced oysters. The menu offers inventive delicacies like their renowned brown butter lobster roll in addition to an extensive assortment of raw bar items like oysters, clams, and crudo. It's ideal for a laid-back dinner with friends or a memorable night out because of the sophisticated yet easy-going atmosphere.

What to Try: Eventide's trademark dish, the brown butter lobster roll, reinvents the classic with a luxurious twist. Don't miss it.

Rockland's Primo

Address: 2 S. Main Street; Phone: +1 207-596-0770; Rockland, ME 04841

A hidden farm-to-table gem in the centre of Rockland is Primo. James Beard Award winner Chef Melissa Kelly oversees the kitchen and is dedicated to using foods that are produced locally and sustainably. The eatery runs its own farm, supplying fresh meats, eggs, and fruit that are heavily incorporated into the meals. The menu rotates seasonally to showcase the best that Maine has to offer. The restaurant's cozy and welcoming atmosphere is further enhanced by the quaint farmhouse setting, which includes gardens and greenhouses.

What to Try: Primo's farm-fresh ingredients are showcased in the house-made pasta, which is a seasonal highlight.

The Kennebunkport Clam Shack

Address: 2 Western Avenue; Phone: +1 207-967-3321; Kennebunkport, ME 04046

The Clam Shack in Kennebunkport is a must-visit if you want a real Maine experience. For many years, this well-known seafood stand has been providing Maine with some of the best lobster rolls. Made with fresh lobster meat and your choice of mayonnaise or butter, the Clam Shack's lobster roll is uncomplicated yet delicious, served on a soft, toasted bun. Both locals and visitors adore it because of the laid-back, informal ambiance. During the busiest time of year, there are usually queues at this well-liked location, so arrive early.

What to Try: Obviously, the lobster roll! Worth the trek, this meal embodies all that is Maine.

Earth at Kennebunkport near Hidden Pond

Phone: (207) 967-6550;

Address: 354 Goose Rocks Road, Kennebunkport, ME 04046

Nestled in the heart of Kennebunkport's woodlands, Earth at Hidden Pond presents an opulent yet rustic dining experience. Every dish at the restaurant reflects the farm-to-fork concept, with ingredients coming from organic gardens and regional suppliers. With an open kitchen, a wood-fired oven, and outside sitting beneath the stars, the scene is quite magnificent. Earth's menu features a fusion of modern and traditional flavours, with a focus on sustainably farmed fish and seasonal veggies.

What to Try: The wood-fired flatbreads are particularly good; they have the ideal ratio of fresh toppings to crispiness.

Jordan's Farm Well in Cape Elizabeth

Address: 21 Wells Road;

Phone: +1 207-831-9350; Cape Elizabeth, ME 04107

A genuine farm-to-table eating experience may be found at Jordan's Farm's The Well, a hidden treasure. Located in a serene, rustic environment on a working farm in Cape Elizabeth, the restaurant offers outdoor seating. The menu is always rotating, based on what the farm and other suppliers have in stock and what's fresh. The recipes at The Well are straightforward, highlighting the excellence of the ingredients. Even for a laid-back evening with friends, dining here feels like a special occasion.

What to Try: A carefully chosen assortment of the farm's finest produce and regional components may be found on the seasonal tasting menu.

The Two Lights Lobster Shack in Cape Elizabeth

Address: 225 Two Lights Road; Phone: +1 207-799-1677; Cape Elizabeth, Maine 04107

Situated on the brink of the Atlantic, The Lobster Shack at Two Lights boasts stunning views of the sea and some of Maine's greatest seafood. For more than five decades, this beloved family-run eatery has been a favourite for its chowder, fried clams, and famous lobster rolls. The dining area outside is a great spot to eat while taking in the view of the waves crashing against the rocks. It's a classic Maine eating experience that embodies the seaside's beauty and flavour.

What to Try: The whole steamed lobster entrée, which comes with coleslaw on the side and corn on the cob.

Portland's Fore Street

Address: 288 Fore Street; Phone: (207) 775-2717; Portland, ME 04101

Pioneering Portland's culinary scene, Fore Street is renowned for its wood-fired cooking and emphasis on regional products. A wood-fired oven, grill, and turnspit at the middle of the restaurant's open kitchen create a cozy and welcoming ambiance. You can always count on a selection of expertly prepared meats, seafood, and vegetables; however the menu is always changing daily to reflect what's freshest from nearby farms and fisheries. Fore Street has garnered a devoted following and multiple accolades due to its unwavering commitment to quality and sustainability.

What to Try: You must try the wood-grilled Maine mussels, which come with bread for dipping and garlic-almond butter.

Camden's Francine Bistro

Phone: +1 207-230-0083; Address: 55 Chestnut Street, Camden, ME 04843.

MAP

Made in the USA
Monee, IL
27 December 2024

75548509R00046